A

Betty Crocker
PICTURE COOKBOOK

All Kinds of
SALADS

GOLDEN PRESS/NEW YORK
Western Publishing Company, Inc.
Racine, Wisconsin

CONTENTS

Main Dish

Beef Plate	**5**
Brussels Salad	**6**
Layered Salad	**7**
Creamy Dried Beef Mold	**8**
Tongue Salad	**9**
Ham-Potato Salad	**10**
Ham-Rice Medley	**11**
Ham-Fruit Ring	**12**
Salad Submarine	**14**
Picnic Toss	**15**
Hot Dog Salad	**15**
Lemon Barbecue Chicken Salad	**16**
Chicken Salad	**17**
Tostadas	**19**
Far East Salad	**20**
Turkey Salad for a Crowd	**21**
Tuna Fiesta	**22**
Tuna Slaw	**23**
Broiled Lettuce Salads	**24**
Seafood Choice Salad	**27**
Florida Salad	**28**
Egg-Nut Salad	**29**
Egg-Bean Salad	**30**
Jellied Beans	**30**

Vegetable

Spinach-Bacon Flambé   33
Wilted Lettuce and Salami   34
Glossy Greens   34
Caesar Salad   36
Freezer Coleslaw   39
Garden Slaw   40
Sweet Slaw/Bean Slaw   41
Greek Salad   42
Tri-Bean Mix   43
Down Home Potato Salad   44
Sweet Potato Salad   46
Tomato Plate   47
Guacamole Salad   49
Cucumber Soufflé Salad   50

Fruit

Fruit Salad Hawaiian   52
Avocado Salads/Pear Waldorf   54
Arizona Salad/Sesame Fruit   55
Mallow Fruits/Cherry Mold   57
Tequila Salad   58
Cherry-Olive Salad   60
Apple Mold   61
Daiquiri Salad   63
Apple Cider Salad   64

Spoon beef mixture onto lettuce; top with onion rings.

Arrange the reserved corned beef on side of lettuce.

Add the drained green beans.

Top mixture with anchovies.

Beef Plate

2 packages (3 ounces each) sliced corned
   beef or sliced smoked beef
1 can (8 ounces) whole new potatoes, cut
   into ¼-inch strips
1 can (4 ounces) mushroom stems and
   pieces, drained
1 medium green pepper, cut into ¼-inch
   strips
1 small onion, sliced (reserve 6 rings)
1 medium stalk celery, coarsely chopped
1 medium dill pickle, chopped
½ cup Italian salad dressing
   Lettuce leaves
1 can (16 ounces) whole green beans,
   drained
¼ teaspoon dried thyme leaves
1 can (2 ounces) anchovies, drained
6 spiced peaches

Reserve 1 package corned beef. Snip remaining beef into
small pieces. Mix beef pieces, potatoes, mushrooms, green
pepper, onion slices, celery and pickle. Add dressing; toss.
Refrigerate at least 6 hours.

Arrange lettuce on 6 plates. Spoon beef mixture onto lettuce; top with onion rings. Place reserved beef and the
beans around lettuce. Sprinkle with thyme; top with anchovies. Garnish with peaches and parsley.   6 SERVINGS.

Brussels Salad

---

 1 package (10 ounces) frozen Brussels sprouts
¼ cup vinegar
¼ cup vegetable oil
 1 teaspoon salt
½ teaspoon caraway seed
¼ teaspoon pepper
 1 medium cucumber, sliced
10 cherry tomatoes, cut in half
 4 lettuce cups
12 ounces corned beef, cut into thin slices

Cook Brussels sprouts as directed on package; drain. Shake vinegar, oil, salt, caraway seed and pepper in tightly covered container. Pour dressing on hot Brussels sprouts and cucumber, tossing to coat evenly. Cover and refrigerate at least 3 hours.

Just before serving, add tomatoes and toss. Spoon into lettuce cups; garnish with snipped parsley. Arrange corned beef slices beside lettuce cups.　　4 SERVINGS.

Layered Salad

1 large head lettuce, torn into bite-size
   pieces (about 6 cups)
2 jars (2½ ounces each) dried beef, cut up
5 ounces mushrooms, sliced
¼ cup sliced radishes
½ cup mayonnaise or salad dressing
¼ cup dairy sour cream
3 green onions, sliced (about ¼ cup)
¼ teaspoon dried dill weed

Layer half each of the lettuce, beef and mushrooms and the radishes in glass salad bowl. Top with remaining lettuce, beef and mushrooms. Mix mayonnaise, sour cream, onions and dill. Drop by spoonfuls onto salad. Cover and refrigerate 2 hours. Just before serving, toss.   4 OR 5 SERVINGS.

Creamy Dried Beef Mold

 1 envelope unflavored gelatin
½ cup cold water
 1 cup mayonnaise or salad dressing
 1 teaspoon prepared mustard
⅔ cup skim milk
 1 can (8 ounces) lima beans, drained
 1 jar (2½ ounces) dried beef, finely cut up
   (see note)
 2 medium stalks celery, chopped (about 1
   cup)
¼ cup grated American cheese food
 1 tablespoon lemon juice
 2 teaspoons instant minced onion
   Celery leaves

Sprinkle gelatin on cold water in saucepan to soften; stir over low heat until gelatin is dissolved. Remove from heat. Mix mayonnaise and mustard in medium bowl; beat in gelatin mixture. Stir in milk. Cover and refrigerate until slightly thickened, 30 to 45 minutes.

Stir in beans, beef, celery, cheese, lemon juice and onion. Pour into 4-cup mold. Refrigerate until firm, about 3 hours. Unmold and garnish with celery leaves.   4 TO 6 SERVINGS.

Note: If dried beef is too salty, pour boiling water on it and drain.

If dried beef is too salty, pour boiling water on it.

Refrigerate gelatin mixture until slightly thickened.

Dip tomatoes into boiling water 1 minute, then into cold.

Use a sharp paring knife to peel off the skin easily.

Cut the tomatoes into eighths.

Spoon mixture into tomatoes.

Tongue Salad

- **6 medium tomatoes**
- **½ teaspoon salt**
- **½ cup mayonnaise or salad dressing**
- **2 tablespoons chopped onion**
- **½ teaspoon dried tarragon leaves**
- **2 cups cut-up cooked tongue**
- **6 slices bacon, crisply fried and crumbled**
- **1 medium stalk celery, thinly sliced**
- **6 lettuce cups**

Peel tomatoes and cut into eighths, cutting to within 1 inch of bottoms as pictured. Spread sections carefully; sprinkle with salt. Mix mayonnaise, onion and tarragon. Toss with tongue, bacon and celery; spoon tongue mixture into tomatoes. Serve in lettuce cups.   6 SERVINGS.

9

Ham-Potato Salad

- 1 package (5.5 ounces) hash brown potatoes with onions
- ½ pound canned ham, cut into bite-size pieces (about 2 cups)
- ½ pound sharp American cheese, cut into ¼-inch cubes
- 6 green onions (with tops), sliced (about ½ cup)
- 1 medium stalk celery, coarsely chopped (about ½ cup)
- ½ small green pepper, coarsely chopped (about ¼ cup)
- ½ cup mayonnaise or salad dressing
- ½ teaspoon salt
- ¼ teaspoon paprika
  Lettuce cups

Pour enough boiling water on potatoes to cover; let stand 10 minutes. Drain completely. Mix potatoes with remaining ingredients except lettuce cups. Cover and refrigerate 2 hours; spoon into lettuce cups.   5 or 6 SERVINGS.

Pour enough boiling water on potatoes to cover; let stand 10 minutes. Drain completely.

Mix with ham, cheese, onions, celery, green pepper, mayonnaise, salt and paprika.

Don't throw away those celery tops! Separate the leaves from the stalks and add them fresh to salads or use them on cooked vegetables as a garnish. Or dry them and use in stuffings for pork chops, chicken or turkey. Small stalks can be chopped and added to sandwich fillings, cooked peas, soups or casseroles.

Ham-Rice Medley

1 tablespoon mayonnaise or salad dressing
½ teaspoon salt
¼ teaspoon cayenne red pepper
⅛ teaspoon paprika
2 cups cubed canned ham
1 can (16 ounces) Spanish rice
1 can (15 ounces) garbanzo beans, drained
2 medium stalks celery, sliced (about 1 cup)
½ medium green pepper, chopped (½ cup)
1 tablespoon instant minced onion
Lettuce leaves
Celery leaves (optional)

Mix mayonnaise, salt, red pepper and paprika. Add ham, rice, beans, celery, green pepper and onion; toss. Refrigerate about 3 hours. Spoon into lettuce-lined bowl and garnish with celery leaves.   5 OR 6 SERVINGS.

Ham-Fruit Ring

    1 medium pineapple
    ½ pound canned ham, cut into bite-size
        pieces
    2 medium stalks celery, sliced (about 1 cup)
    1 cup seedless grapes
    ¾ cup mayonnaise or salad dressing
    2 teaspoons lemon juice
    ½ teaspoon ground ginger
    ⅛ teaspoon garlic salt
    ½ cup chopped salted peanuts or slivered
        almonds
      Lettuce leaves
      Seedless grapes

Remove top from pineapple; cut pineapple crosswise into
4 or 5 slices. Cut pineapple from each slice, leaving ½-inch
ring as pictured; reserve rings. Core and cut up pineapple.
Toss 2 cups of the pineapple with the ham, celery and 1 cup
grapes.

Mix mayonnaise, lemon juice, ginger and garlic salt; toss
with ham mixture. Just before serving, fold in peanuts.
Arrange reserved pineapple rings on lettuce leaves; fill
with ham mixture. Garnish with grapes.   4 OR 5 SERVINGS.

Remove top from pineapple; cut crosswise into slices.

Cut the pineapple from each slice, leaving ½-inch ring.

Salad Submarine

3 packages (3 ounces each) sliced smoked
   ham
2 large stalks celery, thinly sliced (about
   1½ cups)
¾ cup chopped sweet pickle
¾ cup mayonnaise or salad dressing
1 loaf (1 pound) unsliced Vienna bread
¼ cup butter or margarine, softened
1 teaspoon prepared mustard
   Cherry tomatoes
   Celery leaves

Reserve 6 slices smoked ham; finely snip remaining slices.
Mix ham pieces, celery, pickle and mayonnaise. Refrigerate about 1 hour.

Cut thin slice from top of loaf; scoop out inside, leaving
¾-inch wall. Mix butter and mustard; spread over inside
of loaf. Line loaf with reserved ham slices; fill with ham
mixture. Garnish with tomatoes and celery leaves. Just
before serving, cut into slices.　　6 SERVINGS.

Cut a thin slice from the top of
loaf; scoop out the inside, leaving a ¾-inch wall.

Line loaf with the reserved
ham slices and fill with the
ham mixture. Garnish.

Picnic Toss

1 can (18 ounces) fully cooked ham, cut into
½-inch cubes (about 4 cups)
1 can (14 ounces) baked beans with tomato
sauce, drained
2 medium stalks celery, sliced (about 1 cup)
½ cup sweet pickle strips
½ cup mayonnaise or salad dressing
2 teaspoons prepared mustard
1 can (8 ounces) pineapple chunks in juice,
chilled and drained

Toss ham, beans, celery and pickle. Mix mayonnaise and mustard; toss with ham mixture. Cover and refrigerate until chilled, about 3 hours. Garnish with pineapple.
6 TO 8 SERVINGS.

Hot Dog Salad

½ cup Italian salad dressing
¼ cup catsup
1 tablespoon instant minced onion
1½ teaspoons prepared mustard
1 package (16 ounces) frankfurters, sliced
½ pound small zucchini, cut diagonally into
slices (about 2 cups)
1 can (8 ounces) whole new potatoes, cut
into fourths
1 medium carrot, cut into bite-size pieces
Lettuce cups
Grated American cheese food

Mix salad dressing, catsup, onion and mustard. Stir in frankfurters, zucchini, potatoes and carrot. Cover and refrigerate 3 hours, stirring occasionally. Serve in lettuce cups; sprinkle with cheese.   4 SERVINGS.

Lemon Barbecue Chicken Salad

2 cups cut-up cooked chicken or turkey,
  chilled
1 tablespoon lemon juice
½ teaspoon salt
2 cups cooked rice, chilled
2 large stalks celery, sliced (about 1½ cups)
½ cup sliced pimiento-stuffed olives
  Barbecue Dressing (below)
3 tablespoons bacon-flavored vegetable
  protein chips

Sprinkle chicken with lemon juice and salt. Add rice, celery, olives and Barbecue Dressing; toss. Sprinkle with protein chips and garnish with parsley sprigs.   5 SERVINGS.

BARBECUE DRESSING
Mix ¾ cup mayonnaise or salad dressing, 1 tablespoon barbecue sauce and ¼ teaspoon liquid smoke.

A cooked 2-pound broiler-fryer yields about 2 cups cut-up chicken for the salad.

Cook chicken up to 24 hours ahead. Cool quickly; remove skin. Cut up and refrigerate.

Chicken Salad

2 cups cut-up cooked chicken
1 can (16 ounces) cut green beans, drained
1 can (15½ ounces) kidney beans, drained
1 can (14 ounces) artichoke hearts, drained
    and cut in half
1 package (4 ounces) sunflower nuts
½ head lettuce, torn into bite-size pieces
    Snipped parsley
    Few drops red pepper sauce
⅔ cup Italian salad dressing

Arrange chicken, beans, artichoke hearts and sunflower nuts on lettuce on tray. Sprinkle chicken with parsley. Mix pepper sauce and salad dressing; drizzle ⅓ cup over the beans. Have your guests assemble their own salads and toss with the remaining dressing.   6 SERVINGS.

Crumble 2 tostada shells on each of 6 salad plates.

Layer half the chicken pieces on crumbled tostadas.

Then top chicken with half of the Mexican Coleslaw.

Add cheese and the remaining chicken and coleslaw.

Tostadas

1 package (5 ounces) tostada shells (12)
2 packages (3 ounces each) sliced smoked
    chicken, cut up
  Mexican Coleslaw (below)
1 cup shredded Cheddar cheese (4 ounces)
½ cup sliced pitted ripe olives
1 orange, pared and cut into 6 wedges
  Chili powder
  Taco sauce

Crumble 2 tostada shells on each of 6 salad plates. Layer half each of the chicken pieces and Mexican Coleslaw on crumbled tostadas. Top with cheese, remaining chicken and coleslaw, the olives and orange wedges. Sprinkle with chili powder; top with taco sauce.   6 SERVINGS.

MEXICAN COLESLAW
1 small head cabbage, shredded
1 small green pepper, chopped (½ cup)
½ cup chopped pimiento
3 green onions (with tops), thinly sliced
½ cup unflavored yogurt
½ teaspoon seasoned salt
½ teaspoon celery seed

Mix all ingredients. Refrigerate 1 hour.

Far East Salad

Romaine leaves
2 packages (2½ ounces each) sliced smoked chicken
1 small green pepper, cut into bite-size pieces
1 can (8½ ounces) water chestnuts, drained and cut in half
2 jars (4 ounces each) whole pimiento, drained and cut into thirds
3 medium stalks celery, cut diagonally into 1-inch slices
1 medium carrot, cut diagonally into thin slices
1 large mild onion, cut crosswise in half, then into thin wedges
1 can (4½ ounces) sliced mushrooms, drained
Ginger Dressing (below)

Arrange romaine leaves on large platter. Arrange remaining ingredients except Ginger Dressing on romaine. Serve with dressing.   6 SERVINGS.

GINGER DRESSING

Mix ⅔ cup French salad dressing, 1 small clove garlic, 2 teaspoons soy sauce, 2 teaspoons molasses and ¼ to ½ teaspoon ground ginger. Refrigerate 2 to 3 hours. Remove garlic before serving.

Turkey Salad for a Crowd

12 cups cut-up cooked turkey
 8 medium stalks celery, sliced (about 4 cups)
 3 jars (10 ounces each) watermelon pickles,
     drained and cut into fourths
 1 medium onion, chopped (about ½ cup)
 3 cups mayonnaise or salad dressing
 4 teaspoons salt
 2 teaspoons curry powder
 ¼ teaspoon freshly ground pepper
 4 cups chow mein noodles
   Celery leaves

Divide turkey, celery, pickles and onion between 2 large bowls. Mix mayonnaise, salt, curry powder and pepper. Toss half of the mayonnaise mixture gently with each turkey mixture. Refrigerate no longer than 12 hours.

Just before serving, stir half of the noodles into each turkey mixture. Garnish with celery leaves.   18 SERVINGS.

TALKING TURKEY

A 5- to 6-pound turkey roast will yield about 12 cups cut-up turkey. Bake as directed on package.

A 12-pound turkey will yield about 14 cups cut-up turkey. To poach, cut turkey into quarters; place in enough water to cover bottom of large kettle. Sprinkle with 2 tablespoons salt and 2 teaspoons white pepper. Heat to boiling; reduce heat. Cover and simmer until turkey is done, 2 to 2½ hours.

Remove turkey from broth; refrigerate at least 1 hour but no longer than 2 days. Remove meat from bones and cut up.

Score cucumber before slicing to make a notched edge.

Cut green pepper crosswise to make attractive rings.

Tuna Fiesta

Yogurt Dressing (below)
Salad greens
2 cans (6½ ounces each) tuna, drained and
   flaked
2 medium tomatoes, cut into wedges
1 medium cucumber, scored and thinly sliced
1 medium green pepper, cut into rings
1 cup cheese-flavored croutons
   Bacon-flavored vegetable protein chips

Prepare Yogurt Dressing. Arrange greens on large platter. Arrange tuna, tomatoes, cucumber, green pepper and croutons on greens. Spoon 2 tablespoons Yogurt Dressing onto tuna; sprinkle with protein chips. Serve with remaining Yogurt Dressing.   4 TO 6 SERVINGS.

YOGURT DRESSING
Mix ⅓ cup unflavored yogurt, 1 teaspoon instant minced onion and ¼ cup mayonnaise or salad dressing thoroughly.

Tuna Slaw

4 ounces uncooked elbow macaroni (about
  1 cup)
½ small head cabbage, shredded
1 medium cucumber, cut into ¼-inch pieces
1 small onion, chopped (about ¼ cup)
½ cup mayonnaise or salad dressing
½ teaspoon salt
¼ teaspoon pepper
1 can (9¾ ounces) tuna, drained and flaked
  Radish fans
  Parsley sprigs

Cook macaroni as directed on package. Rinse under run-
ning cold water; drain. Mix macaroni, cabbage, cucumber,
onion, mayonnaise, salt and pepper. Stir in tuna. Refrigerate at least 3 hours. Garnish with radish fans and parsley
sprigs.   6 SERVINGS.

 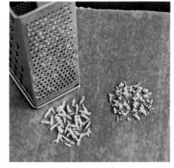

For grated peel, rub only outer
yellow part, using short
strokes on fine side of grater.

For shredded peel, use the
slightly coarser side of grater.
Shred only outer yellow part.

Broiled Lettuce Salads

Cut three 1-inch slices from center of each of 2 medium heads lettuce; place on ungreased baking sheet. Top with Shrimp Topping or Pizza Topping (below). Set oven control to broil and/or 550°. Broil with tops 4 to 5 inches from heat until cheese starts to brown, about 3 minutes.   6 SERVINGS.

SHRIMP TOPPING
- ¾ cup mayonnaise or salad dressing
- 1 unpared small cucumber, thinly sliced
- 1 can (4½ ounces) tiny shrimp, drained
  Garlic salt
- ⅓ cup grated Parmesan cheese

Spread each lettuce slice with 2 tablespoons of the mayonnaise. Top with cucumber and shrimp; sprinkle with garlic salt and cheese.

PIZZA TOPPING
- ½ cup tomato sauce
- ¼ cup vegetable oil
- 1 tablespoon red wine vinegar
- ½ teaspoon garlic salt
- ¼ teaspoon dried basil leaves
- ¼ teaspoon dried oregano leaves
- 1 can (8 ounces) kidney beans, drained
- ½ cup chopped salami (about 3 ounces)
- 3 green onions, chopped (about ⅓ cup)
- ¾ cup shredded mozzarella cheese (about 3 ounces)
- ⅓ cup grated Parmesan cheese

Shake tomato sauce, oil, vinegar, garlic salt, basil and oregano in covered container; spread each lettuce slice with 2 tablespoons of the tomato mixture. Top with beans, salami, onions and mozzarella cheese. Sprinkle with Parmesan cheese.

Cut three 1-inch crosswise slices from center of each head of lettuce.

Spread lettuce slices with tomato mixture; top with remaining ingredients.

Mix shrimp, scallops, pepper,
mushrooms, lemon and onion.

Mix marinade; pour it on the
shrimp mixture. Refrigerate.

Stir parsley into marinade reserved from drained shrimp.

Serve shrimp mixture, lettuce
and the marinade separately.

Seafood Choice Salad

1 package (12 ounces) frozen cooked shrimp,
    thawed (2 cups)
½ pound scallops, cooked and drained
1 medium green pepper, cut into ¼-inch
    strips
½ pound mushrooms, sliced
1 medium lemon, cut into wedges
1 medium onion, sliced and separated into
    rings
⅔ cup tarragon vinegar
½ cup vegetable oil
1 teaspoon sugar
1 teaspoon salt
⅛ teaspoon dried tarragon leaves
1 bay leaf, crumbled
1 teaspoon snipped parsley
1 small head lettuce, torn into bite-size
    pieces
  Salt
  Coarsely ground pepper

Mix shrimp, scallops, green pepper, mushrooms, lemon and onion in baking dish, 13½x8¾x1¾ inches. Mix vinegar, oil, sugar, 1 teaspoon salt, tarragon and bay leaf; pour on shrimp mixture. Cover and refrigerate 8 hours, spooning marinade onto shrimp mixture occasionally.

Drain shrimp mixture, reserving marinade. Stir parsley into marinade. Serve shrimp mixture, lettuce and reserved marinade in separate bowls. Your guests can make and toss their own salads, then season them with salt and pepper.   6 TO 8 SERVINGS.

To make your own cocktail sauce, mix 1 cup chili sauce and 2 teaspoons horseradish.

Add 2 teaspoons lemon juice, ½ teaspoon Worcestershire sauce and ⅛ teaspoon salt.

Florida Salad

1 large head lettuce, shredded
2 avocados, peeled and sliced
1 tablespoon lemon juice
2 cans (4½ ounces each) tiny deveined
   shrimp, rinsed and drained
4 ounces Cheddar cheese, cut into ¼-inch
   strips
12 cherry tomatoes, cut in half
1 medium unpared cucumber, scored and
   thinly sliced
1 cup shrimp cocktail sauce
3 tablespoons mayonnaise or salad dressing

Arrange lettuce in large salad bowl. Drizzle avocados with lemon juice. Arrange avocados, shrimp, cheese, tomatoes and cucumber on lettuce. Mix cocktail sauce and mayonnaise; serve with salad.   6 TO 8 SERVINGS.

Egg-Nut Salad

4 hard-cooked eggs, chopped
2 medium stalks celery, sliced
1 cup shredded process American cheese
½ cup mayonnaise or salad dressing
¼ cup chopped salted peanuts
¼ teaspoon onion salt
⅛ teaspoon dry mustard
   Lettuce cups

Mix eggs, celery, cheese, mayonnaise, peanuts, onion salt and mustard. Cover and refrigerate 1½ hours. Mound mixture in lettuce cups.   4 SERVINGS.

To peel eggs, cool in water.

Tap to crack the egg shells.

Roll between hands to loosen.

Peel eggs under cold water.

Egg-Bean Salad

1 can (16 ounces) kidney beans, drained
½ pound Swiss cheese, cut into ½-inch cubes
    (about 1½ cups)
½ cup Italian salad dressing
1 medium stalk celery, chopped (about
    ½ cup)
1 small onion, chopped (about ¼ cup)
6 lettuce cups
3 hard-cooked eggs, cut into fourths

Toss beans, cheese, salad dressing, celery and onion. Refrigerate at least 2 hours but no longer than 24 hours. Serve in lettuce cups and garnish with eggs.   6 SERVINGS.

Jellied Beans

2½ cups boiling water
1 package (6 ounces) lemon-flavored gelatin
1 teaspoon onion salt
¼ cup vinegar
1 can (16 ounces) lima beans, drained
1 can (8 ounces) kidney beans, drained
1 jar (2 ounces) sliced pimiento, drained
⅔ cup chopped pecans
3 tablespoons chopped dill pickle
2 cups shredded Swiss cheese (8 ounces)
    Leaf lettuce

Pour boiling water on gelatin and onion salt in large bowl; stir until gelatin is dissolved. Stir in vinegar. Refrigerate until slightly thickened, about 1½ hours.

Stir lima beans, kidney beans, pimiento, pecans and pickle into gelatin mixture; pour into 6 individual molds. Refrigerate until firm, about 4 hours. Place ⅓ cup cheese on each serving of lettuce; top with gelatin.   6 SERVINGS.

To hard-cook eggs, pour cold water 1 inch above eggs; heat to boiling. Remove from heat.

Cover and let stand 22 to 24 minutes. Quickly cool eggs in cold water to stop cooking.

Or first place uncooked eggs in warm water to warm so the shells won't crack.

Then transfer eggs to boiling water; cook 20 minutes below simmering and cool quickly.

Heat bacon fat-honey-vinegar mixture; pour on spinach and mushrooms. Toss.

Squeeze lemon over the salad, then ignite bacon and brandy and pour on salad.

Spinach-Bacon Flambé

    6 slices bacon, cut into ½-inch pieces
    2 tablespoons honey
    2 tablespoons red wine vinegar
1½ teaspoons Worcestershire sauce
    ¼ teaspoon salt
  10 ounces spinach, torn into bite-size pieces
    5 ounces mushrooms, sliced
    1 lemon, cut in half
    ¼ cup brandy

Fry bacon in skillet until crisp. Remove from skillet; drain on paper towel. Drain skillet, reserving 2 tablespoons bacon fat. Heat reserved bacon fat, honey, vinegar, Worcestershire sauce and salt just to boiling. Pour mixture on spinach and mushrooms; toss. Squeeze lemon over salad.

Heat bacon pieces and brandy in small skillet or saucepan just until warm. Ignite and pour on salad. Toss gently; serve immediately.   6 SERVINGS.

VIVE LA FLAMBE!

Flaming foods are special and they look spectacular. Do you know how easy it is? Just start with hot food and an 80-proof liquor such as rum, brandy or a fruit-flavored liqueur. Heat the liquor in a small long-handled pan, then ignite carefully—long matches are recommended—and pour the flaming liquid over the food and stir. The alcohol burns off but the flavor remains. Dim the lights and you're set for another hit!

Wilted Lettuce and Salami

4 ounces sliced salami, cut into 8 wedges
¼ cup vinegar
3 tablespoons vegetable oil
2 teaspoons sugar
1 teaspoon dried oregano leaves
¼ teaspoon salt
⅛ teaspoon pepper
1 small head lettuce, torn into bite-size
    pieces (about 4 cups)
1 small bunch romaine, torn into bite-size
    pieces (about 4 cups)
1 medium apple, sliced
1 small green pepper, chopped (about ¼
    cup)

Cook and stir salami in electric skillet or wok until light
brown, about 5 minutes. Stir in vinegar, oil, sugar, oregano,
salt and pepper. Heat just to boiling; turn off heat. Add
lettuce, romaine, apple and green pepper; toss gently.
Serve immediately.   8 SERVINGS.

Glossy Greens

6 ounces spinach, torn into bite-size pieces
3 tablespoons crumbled blue cheese
3 tablespoons French salad dressing
¾ cup garlic-and-onion-flavored croutons

Toss spinach, cheese and salad dressing. Sprinkle with
croutons.   4 OR 5 SERVINGS.

Cook and stir salami until light brown, about 5 minutes.

Stir in vinegar, oil, sugar and seasonings, then heat.

Add lettuce, romaine, apple and green pepper.

Toss gently until salad greens are well coated.

Caesar Salad

1 clove garlic, cut in half
⅓ cup olive oil
1 teaspoon Worcestershire sauce
½ teaspoon salt
¼ teaspoon dry mustard
1 large bunch romaine, chilled and torn into
   bite-size pieces (about 12 cups)
   Coddled Egg (right)
1 lemon, cut in half
   Onion-Cheese Croutons (right)
¼ cup grated Parmesan cheese
   Freshly ground pepper
1 can (about 2 ounces) anchovy fillets,
   drained and cut up

Just before serving, rub large salad bowl with garlic. Place garlic in oil; let stand 5 minutes. Discard garlic. Mix oil, Worcestershire sauce, salt and mustard. Place romaine in salad bowl. Pour oil mixture on top; toss. Break Coddled Egg onto romaine; squeeze lemon over salad. Toss until leaves are well coated. Sprinkle with Onion-Cheese Croutons, cheese, pepper and anchovies; toss.　　6 SERVINGS.

Pour oil mixture on romaine in a large salad bowl.

Toss romaine with oil mixture until leaves glisten.

Break Coddled Egg onto the romaine; squeeze lemon over the salad and toss.

Sprinkle salad with croutons, cheese, freshly ground pepper and anchovies; toss.

CODDLED EGG

To prevent cold egg from cracking, place in warm water. Heat enough water to completely cover egg to boiling. Transfer egg to boiling water. Remove from heat; cover and let stand 30 seconds. Immediately cool egg in cold water; refrigerate.

ONION-CHEESE CROUTONS

Heat oven to 400°. Trim crusts from 4 slices white bread: butter both sides. Mix ¼ teaspoon onion powder and 1½ tablespoons grated Parmesan cheese; sprinkle over bread. Cut bread into ½-inch cubes; place in ungreased shallow baking pan. Bake, stirring occasionally, until golden brown and crisp, 10 to 15 minutes.

Shred 1 medium head cabbage.

Spoon mixture into containers.

Freezer Coleslaw

1 medium head cabbage, shredded (about
    5 cups)
1 teaspoon salt
2 cups sugar
1 cup vinegar
½ cup water
1 teaspoon celery seed
4 medium stalks celery, chopped (about
    2 cups)
1 small green pepper, chopped (about ½
    cup)
1 medium carrot, cut lengthwise into fourths
    and thinly sliced (about ½ cup)
1 small onion, chopped (about ¼ cup)

Mix cabbage and salt; let stand 1 hour. Heat sugar, vinegar, water and celery seed to boiling in 1-quart saucepan. Boil and stir 1 minute. Cool to lukewarm.

Drain cabbage; stir in celery, green pepper, carrot and onion. Stir vinegar mixture into cabbage mixture. Spoon into three 1-pint freezer containers. Cover and label; freeze up to 1 month.

∎8 hours before serving, place in refrigerator to thaw. Drain well before serving. Garnish with sliced pimiento-stuffed olives.　　6 CUPS COLESLAW.

Toss remaining onion rings with the other vegetables.

Heat the dressing ingredients and toss with the slaw.

Garden Slaw

1 small onion, sliced and separated into
    rings
½ medium head cabbage, chopped
2 medium stalks celery, chopped (about 1
    cup)
1 medium carrot, shredded (about ½ cup)
1 medium zucchini, sliced
¼ cup sugar
¼ cup vinegar
¼ cup vegetable oil
1 teaspoon celery seed
½ teaspoon salt
½ teaspoon dry mustard
    Dash of pepper

Reserve a few onion rings. Toss remaining onion rings, the cabbage, celery, carrot and zucchini. Heat remaining ingredients to boiling; boil and stir 1 minute. Toss with vegetables. Refrigerate 3 hours, stirring occasionally. Garnish with reserved onion rings.   8 SERVINGS.

Sweet Slaw

1 can (8 ounces) sliced peaches, drained
1 cup shredded cabbage (about ⅓ small
   head)
1 small carrot, shredded (about ¼ cup)
½ cup miniature marshmallows
3 to 4 tablespoons mayonnaise or salad
   dressing
1 teaspoon lemon juice
   Lettuce leaves

Reserve 4 peach slices. Cut remaining peaches into ½-inch pieces; mix with cabbage, carrot, marshmallows, mayonnaise and lemon juice. Refrigerate 1 hour; serve over lettuce and garnish with reserved peach slices.   4 SERVINGS.

Bean Slaw

⅓ cup sugar
⅓ cup vinegar
3 tablespoons vegetable oil
¼ teaspoon salt
   Dash of pepper
2 cups chopped cabbage
1 can (16 ounces) cut green beans, drained
1 can (15½ ounces) cut wax beans, drained
1 small onion, sliced

Mix sugar, vinegar, oil, salt and pepper. Toss with cabbage, beans and onion. Refrigerate about 2 hours.
5 OR 6 SERVINGS.

Pour the salad dressing on the olives and vegetables.

Place romaine and lettuce on top; add cheese and anchovies.

Greek Salad

    1 jar (6½ ounces) Greek black or ripe
      green olives, drained
   10 radishes, sliced (about 1 cup)
    1 medium cucumber, sliced
    6 green onions, cut into ½-inch slices
   ½ cup vegetable oil
   ⅓ cup wine vinegar
  1½ teaspoons salt
  1½ teaspoons dried oregano leaves
    1 medium bunch romaine, torn into
      bite-size pieces
    1 medium head lettuce, torn into bite-size
      pieces
   ¼ cup crumbled blue or feta cheese
    1 can (2 ounces) anchovies, drained

Place olives, radishes, cucumber and onions in 3-quart bowl. Mix oil, vinegar, salt and oregano in covered glass container; shake well. Pour salad dressing on olives and vegetables. Place romaine and lettuce on top; arrange cheese and anchovies on lettuce. Cover and refrigerate at least 2 hours. Just before serving, toss salad.   8 SERVINGS.

Tri-Bean Mix

¼ cup mayonnaise or salad dressing
¼ cup hot dog relish
2 teaspoons prepared horseradish
½ teaspoon dried dill weed
1 can (8 ounces) cut wax beans, drained
1 can (16 ounces) lima beans, drained
1 can (15½ ounces) kidney beans, drained
1 pound bulk bologna, cut into ½-inch
  pieces (about 3½ cups)
1 small onion, chopped (about ¼ cup)
3 medium stalks celery, chopped (1½ cups)
  Spinach or lettuce leaves

Mix mayonnaise, relish, horseradish and dill until blended. Toss with remaining ingredients except spinach leaves. Cover and refrigerate 4 hours. Serve in spinach-lined bowl.   8 SERVINGS.

Mix mayonnaise, hot dog relish, horseradish and dill.

Toss with remaining ingredients except spinach leaves.

Down Home Potato Salad

8 medium new potatoes, cooked, cut into
   ¼-inch cubes and chilled (about 5 cups)
3 large stalks celery, cut into diagonal slices
   (about 2¼ cups)
1 jar (4 ounces) whole pimiento, drained and
   sliced
¼ cup sweet pickle relish
½ small green pepper, chopped (about ¼
   cup)
2 hard-cooked eggs, chopped
2 tablespoons sweet pickle juice
2 teaspoons instant minced onion
½ cup mayonnaise or salad dressing
1 to 2 tablespoons prepared mustard
1 teaspoon seasoned salt
2 hard-cooked eggs, sliced
   Celery leaves

Toss potatoes, celery, pimiento, relish, green pepper and
chopped eggs. Mix pickle juice and onion; let stand 3
minutes. Stir in mayonnaise, mustard and seasoned salt;
toss with potato mixture. Garnish with egg slices and celery leaves.   12 SERVINGS.

Potatoes cut into small pieces
absorb flavors readily.

Ingredients tossed with a light
hand hold their shapes.

Sweet Potato Salad

　　5　cups water
1½　pounds sweet potatoes
　　2　medium stalks celery, thinly sliced (about 1 cup)
　　1　small onion, thinly sliced
　　1　medium orange, peeled and sectioned
　½　cup mayonnaise or salad dressing
　　1　to 2 tablespoons orange or pineapple juice
　½　teaspoon dry mustard
　½　teaspoon grated orange peel
　¼　teaspoon salt
　¼　teaspoon ground ginger
　⅛　teaspoon pepper
　　　Lettuce leaves

Heat water to boiling; add potatoes. Heat to boiling; reduce heat. Cover and simmer until tender, 30 to 35 minutes.

Drain potatoes; slip off skins. Cut potatoes into ½-inch cubes. Add celery, onion and orange. Mix remaining ingredients except lettuce leaves; pour on vegetables and orange. Stir to blend. Refrigerate at least 2 hours. Serve in lettuce-lined salad bowl. 　4 TO 6 SERVINGS.

SWEET POTATOES are a good source of vitamin A and contain some vitamin C. They range from light yellow to deep orange. The latter, called yams, are sweeter and more moist. Sweet potatoes can be baked, boiled or fried. Store in a cool, dry place of 55 to 60° for a short time as they are perishable.

TOMATOES are the most flavorful when picked completely ripe. Look for well-formed tomatoes that are unblemished and smooth; avoid bruised or overripe ones with deep cracks around the stems. For canning and frying, try unripe, mature green tomatoes. For salads or pickles, use cherry or pear tomatoes.

Tomato Plate

½ cup dairy sour cream
¼ teaspoon onion salt
¼ teaspoon garlic salt
   Leaf lettuce
2 medium tomatoes, thinly sliced
1 medium Bermuda onion, sliced
1 small cucumber, sliced

Mix sour cream, onion salt and garlic salt. Arrange lettuce on large platter. Alternate slices of tomatoes, onion and cucumber on lettuce. Spoon dressing onto vegetables.
3 OR 4 SERVINGS.

Sprinkle gelatin on the cold water in saucepan.

Stir over low heat until the gelatin is dissolved.

Mix the avocados and lemon juice in a large bowl.

Stir in gelatin mixture, vegetables and seasonings.

Guacamole Salad

1 tablespoon plus 1 teaspoon unflavored
  gelatin
1½ cups cold water
2 medium avocados, mashed (about 1½
  cups)
¼ cup lemon juice
1 medium stalk celery, thinly sliced (about
  ½ cup)
1 small tomato, peeled and chopped (about
  ½ cup)
2 green onions, chopped (about 3
  tablespoons)
1 to 2 tablespoons chopped canned chilies
1 teaspoon salt
¼ teaspoon red pepper sauce
  Salad greens
  Ripe olives
  Cherry tomatoes

Sprinkle gelatin on ½ cup of the cold water in 1-quart saucepan; stir over low heat until gelatin is dissolved, about 3 minutes. Stir in remaining 1 cup cold water. Refrigerate until slightly thickened, about 40 minutes.

Mix avocados and lemon juice in large bowl. Stir in gelatin mixture, celery, tomato, onions, chilies, salt and pepper sauce. Pour into 4-cup mold. Refrigerate until firm, about 3 hours. Just before serving, unmold on salad greens and garnish with olives and tomatoes.   8 SERVINGS.

Timing Tip: If you want to serve at different times, Guacamole Salad will hold in refrigerator up to 24 hours.

Pour ½ cup of gelatin mixture into mold. Stir the mayonnaise mixture into second gelatin mixture. Add half the vegetables.

Pour vegetable-mayonnaise mixture on first layer. Stir remaining vegetables into reserved gelatin. Pour into mold; refrigerate.

Cucumber Soufflé Salad

- 1 cup boiling water
- 2 packages (3 ounces each) lime-flavored gelatin
- ¾ cup cold water
- 1 cup boiling water
- ½ cup mayonnaise or salad dressing
- ¼ cup cold water
- 2 tablespoons vinegar
- ¼ teaspoon salt
- 1 medium cucumber, chopped (about 1 cup)
- 1 medium stalk celery, thinly sliced (about ½ cup)
- 7 medium radishes, sliced (about ½ cup)

For first layer, pour 1 cup boiling water on 1 package gelatin in bowl; stir until gelatin is dissolved. Stir in ¾ cup cold water. Pour ½ cup of the gelatin mixture into 5-cup mold; refrigerate. Reserve remaining gelatin mixture for third layer.

For second layer, pour 1 cup boiling water on second package gelatin in bowl; stir until gelatin is dissolved. Mix mayonnaise, ¼ cup cold water, the vinegar and salt; stir into gelatin mixture. Refrigerate until slightly thickened, about 1 hour. Stir in half of the cucumber, celery and radishes. Pour on the first layer in mold; refrigerate.

For third layer, refrigerate reserved gelatin until slightly thickened, about 1 hour. Stir in remaining vegetables; pour on second layer in mold. Refrigerate until firm, at least 5 hours.   8 SERVINGS.

Timing Tip: If you want to serve at different times, Cucumber Soufflé Salad will hold in refrigerator up to 24 hours.

To prepare papaya, pare and cut in half; then remove the seeds and cut into slices.

To prepare the mango, score skin into sections; then peel back and cut into slices.

Fruit Salad Hawaiian

Banana Dressing (right)
Ginger Dressing (right)
1 pineapple
1 medium cantaloupe
1 medium honeydew melon
1 papaya, pared and sliced
1 mango, peeled and sliced
2 kiwi fruit, pared and sliced
1 cup green grapes
1 cup strawberries, cut in half
Leaf lettuce

Prepare Banana Dressing and Ginger Dressing. Remove top from pineapple. Cut pineapple in half, then into quarters; cut rind and eyes from quarters. Remove core. Slice quarters into 3x1-inch pieces. Cut balls from cantaloupe and honeydew. Arrange fruit on lettuce. Serve with Banana Dressing and Ginger Dressing.   8 TO 10 SERVINGS.

BANANA DRESSING

    1 banana, sliced
    ½ cup dairy sour cream
    2 tablespoons packed brown sugar
 1½ teaspoons lemon juice

Mix all ingredients in blender container. Cover and blend until smooth, 12 to 15 seconds. Refrigerate 1 hour.

GINGER DRESSING

    ⅓ cup mayonnaise or salad dressing
    ⅓ cup honey
    2 tablespoons chopped crystallized ginger
    1 tablespoon lime juice
    1 tablespoon vegetable oil
    ½ teaspoon grated lime peel

Mix all ingredients; refrigerate 1 hour.

Avocado Salads

3 large avocados
1 can (16 ounces) grapefruit segments,
  drained
1 can (11 ounces) mandarin orange
  segments, drained
1 small banana, thinly sliced
¼ cup honey
2 tablespoons lemon juice
  Leaf lettuce
  Pomegranate seeds (optional)

Cut avocados lengthwise in half; remove pits. Cut fruit from shells with rounded teaspoon or melon ball cutter. Reserve shells. Toss avocado with grapefruit segments, orange segments and banana slices. Mix honey and lemon juice; toss with fruit. Spoon fruit mixture into avocado shells; place on lettuce. Sprinkle with pomegranate seeds. 6 SERVINGS.

Pear Waldorf

4 pears, pared and cut up (about 3 cups)
3 tablespoons orange or pineapple juice
2 medium stalks celery, thinly sliced (about
  1 cup)
½ cup chopped walnuts
½ cup golden raisins
½ cup mayonnaise or salad dressing
  Salad greens
  Celery leaves or sliced pimiento-stuffed
  olives

Sprinkle pears with orange juice. Mix pears, celery, walnuts, raisins and mayonnaise. Serve on salad greens. Garnish with celery leaves.   6 SERVINGS.

Arizona Salad

Arrange avocado slices, mandarin orange segments and sliced bananas on crisp salad greens; sprinkle with coconut. Drizzle with frozen lemonade concentrate, thawed.

Sesame Fruit

½ cup vegetable oil
⅓ cup powdered sugar
2 tablespoons lemon juice
½ teaspoon dry mustard
½ teaspoon salt
½ teaspoon paprika
2 teaspoons sesame seed
1 can (13¼ ounces) pineapple chunks, drained
1 unpared medium apple, coarsely chopped
½ cup green or red grape halves
3 medium bananas
1 medium head lettuce, shredded

Blend oil, sugar, lemon juice, mustard, salt and paprika in small mixer bowl. Beat on medium speed until creamy, 3 to 4 minutes. Stir in sesame seed.

Toss pineapple, apple and grapes. Cut bananas lengthwise in half, then crosswise. Place 2 banana pieces on shredded lettuce on each of 6 salad plates. Spoon fruit into center of bananas. Spoon dressing onto each serving.   6 SERVINGS.

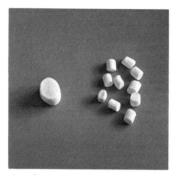

One large marshmallow equals 10 miniature marshmallows.

One cup miniature marshmallows equals 11 or 12 large.

Mallow Fruits

2 cans (11 ounces each) mandarin orange
   segments, drained
1 can (13¼ ounces) pineapple chunks,
   drained
1 jar (4 ounces) maraschino cherries, drained
2 cups miniature marshmallows
1 cup broken walnuts
1 teaspoon lemon juice
1 envelope (2 ounces) whipped topping mix
   Celery leaves

Toss orange segments, pineapple, cherries, marshmallows
and walnuts; drizzle with lemon juice. Prepare topping mix
as directed on package; fold into fruit. Cover and refrigerate 1 hour. Garnish with celery leaves.   8 TO 10 SERVINGS.

Cherry Mold

1 can (16 ounces) pitted dark sweet
   cherries, drained (reserve ¾ cup liquid)
¾ cup water
1 package (6 ounces) raspberry-flavored
   gelatin
1¾ cups strawberry-flavored beverage
½ cup slivered almonds
   Celery leaves
½ cup mayonnaise or salad dressing

Heat reserved cherry liquid and water to boiling. Pour on
gelatin in medium bowl; stir until gelatin is dissolved. Stir
in beverage. Refrigerate until slightly thickened. Stir in
cherries and almonds; pour into 6-cup mold. Refrigerate
until firm, about 4 hours. Garnish with celery leaves and
serve with mayonnaise.   10 SERVINGS.

Tequila Salad

1 can (15¼ ounces) sliced pineapple,
    drained (reserve ¼ cup syrup)
¼ cup lime juice
2 tablespoons powdered sugar
2 tablespoons tequila
2 tablespoons vegetable oil
¼ teaspoon salt
3 medium avocados
    Lime juice
2 large grapefruit
2 large oranges
    Salad greens
    Chopped walnuts
    Salt

Shake reserved pineapple syrup, ¼ cup lime juice, the sugar, tequila, oil and ¼ teaspoon salt in tightly covered container. Refrigerate at least 1 hour.

Cut avocados lengthwise in half; remove pits. Peel avocados; cut into ½-inch pieces. Sprinkle pieces with lime juice. Cut pineapple slices in half. Pare and section grapefruit and oranges; cut sections in half if desired.

Just before serving, toss avocado pieces with pineapple and grapefruit and orange sections; place on salad greens. Sprinkle walnuts and salt over salad. Serve with dressing.
8 SERVINGS.

A salad created from the flavors of the popular Mexican drink, the *Margarita.*

Shake dressing ingredients; refrigerate at least 1 hour.

Toss the fruit just before serving; place on greens.

Cherry-Olive Salad

1 cup boiling water
1 package (3 ounces) cherry-flavored gelatin
1 can (17 ounces) pitted dark sweet cherries,
   drained and cut in half (reserve syrup)
1 tablespoon lemon juice
¼ cup chopped walnuts
¼ cup pimiento-stuffed olives, sliced

Pour boiling water on gelatin in bowl; stir until gelatin is dissolved. Add enough water to reserved cherry syrup to measure ¾ cup. Stir syrup-water mixture and lemon juice into gelatin mixture. Refrigerate until slightly thickened, about 1 hour.

Stir cherries, walnuts and olives into gelatin mixture. Pour into 6 individual molds. Refrigerate until firm, about 3 hours.   6 SERVINGS.

Cherry-Apple Salad: Omit walnuts and olives. Stir 1 medium unpared red apple, chopped (about 1 cup), into slightly thickened gelatin mixture. Divide mixture among 6 individual molds.

Timing Tip: If you want to serve at different times, Cherry-Olive Salad will hold in refrigerator up to 24 hours.

Stir the cherry syrup-water mixture into the dissolved cherry gelatin in bowl.

Stir the cherries, walnuts and olives into the slightly thickened gelatin mixture.

Apple Mold

2½ cups water
 ⅓ cup red cinnamon candies
  1 package (6 ounces) strawberry-flavored
    gelatin
  2 cups applesauce
    Lettuce leaves
    Mayonnaise or salad dressing

Heat water and cinnamon candies, stirring occasionally, until melted. Pour on gelatin in bowl; stir until gelatin is dissolved. Stir in applesauce; pour into 6-cup mold. Refrigerate until firm, 8 to 10 hours. Unmold on lettuce leaves and serve with mayonnaise.   5 OR 6 SERVINGS.

For quick setting, place the gelatin mixture in a container of ice and water; stir often.

Use a melon baller to scoop round uniform balls from the honeydew melon as shown.

Daiquiri Salad

1 cup boiling water
1 package (6 ounces) lime-flavored gelatin
1 can (6 ounces) frozen limeade concentrate
   About ½ cup ginger ale
1 can (20 ounces) pineapple tidbits or
   chunks in juice, drained (reserve juice)
½ cup light rum
   Salad greens
   Honeydew melon balls

Pour boiling water on gelatin in 2-quart bowl; stir until gelatin is dissolved. Stir in frozen concentrate. Add enough ginger ale to reserved pineapple juice to measure 1¼ cups. Stir pineapple juice–ginger ale mixture and rum into gelatin mixture. Refrigerate until slightly thickened, about 1 hour.

Stir in pineapple. Pour into 5-cup mold. Refrigerate until firm, at least 3 hours. Unmold on salad greens. Garnish with melon balls. If desired, serve with whipped topping. 8 TO 10 SERVINGS.

Timing Tip: If you want to serve at different times, Daiquiri Salad will hold in refrigerator up to 24 hours.

Apple Cider Salad

3½ cups apple cider or apple juice
1 package (6 ounces) lemon-flavored gelatin
1 to 2 tablespoons lemon juice
½ teaspoon salt
1 cup Tokay grapes, cut in half and seeded
1 medium stalk celery, chopped (about ½
   cup)
   Salad greens (optional)
   Blue Cheese Mayonnaise (below)

Heat 2 cups of the apple cider to boiling. Pour on gelatin in bowl; stir until gelatin is dissolved. Stir in remaining apple cider, the lemon juice and salt. Refrigerate until slightly thickened, about 1 hour. Stir in grapes and celery. Pour into 6-cup mold. Refrigerate until firm, about 3 hours.

Unmold on salad greens. Serve with Blue Cheese Mayonnaise.   6 SERVINGS.

BLUE CHEESE MAYONNAISE
1 package (3 ounces) cream cheese, softened
¼ cup mayonnaise or salad dressing
2 tablespoons crumbled blue cheese (about 1
   ounce)
2 tablespoons apple cider or apple juice

Mix cream cheese and mayonnaise. Stir in blue cheese and apple cider.

Timing Tip: If you want to serve at different times, Apple Cider Salad and Blue Cheese Mayonnaise will hold in refrigerator up to 24 hours.